READING 2000 ◆ LEVEL ONE ◆ TOPIC

GIFTS

Catherine Allan   Sallie Harkness
James Love   Helen McLullich
Helen Murdoch

Oliver & Boyd

Contents

	page
Notes for the Pupil	2
Gifts	4
The Birthday Gift	5–7
Grandma and Harry	8–10
Thank-you Letters	11, 12
Gift Lists	13, 14
A Gift for a Friend	15
Make your own Wrapping Paper	16
Gifts of a Different Kind	18
Dr Barnardo	20
How can we help?	22
Glossary	23
Review	24

Notes for you and your teacher to talk about

Before you start the work in this book:

1. Read the **title page**.
   It is page 1.
   Find:

   > the title of this book
   > the authors' names.

2. Read the **contents** list.
   It is also on page 1.
   Find:

   > the titles of things to
   > read and do
   > their page numbers.

3. Look quickly through the book. Find a **heading**, for example,

   | Something to do |

   | A story to read |

| READING 2000 ◆ LEVEL ONE ◆ TOPIC READER |

GIFTS

Catherine Allan   Sallie Harkness
James Love   Helen McLullich
          Helen Murdoch

Oliver & Boyd

Contents

	page
Notes for the Pupil	2
Gifts	4
The Birthday Gift	5–7
Grandma and Harry	8–10
Thank-you Letters	11, 12
Gift Lists	13, 14
A Gift for a Friend	15
Make your own Wrapping Paper	16
Gifts of a Different Kind	18
Dr Barnardo	20
How can we help?	22
Glossary	23
Review	24

4. Look at the **glossary**. It is on page 23.
   What does it tell you?

   > The glossary is a small dictionary.
   > It gives the meaning of some words used in this book.
   > The words are in the order of the alphabet.

   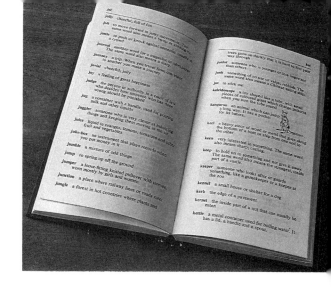

   How should you use it?

   > If you don't know the meaning of a word, first try to find out from the words around it. Then check with the glossary.

5. Discuss and decide.

   > Will you make a booklet for your work?
   > Will you use paper and keep your work neatly in a folder?
   > Will you display your work?

6. Think about these questions:

   > What is a gift?
   > How do **you** choose one?

   Now read 'Gifts'.
   Find its page in the **contents** list.

Gifts

Write and draw. Most people like gifts.
Gifts don't have to cost a lot of money.
It's the kind thought that's important.

If you were asked to choose a gift for each of these people, what would you choose? Think carefully.

1. a new baby

2. a blind person

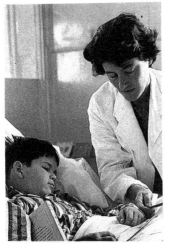
3. someone who looked after your pet while you were on holiday

4. an old lady who lives alone

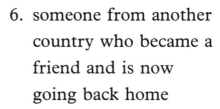
5. someone in hospital

6. someone from another country who became a friend and is now going back home

The Birthday Gift

A story to read

"Mr Rabbit," said the little girl, "I want help."

"Help, little girl, I'll give you help if I can," said Mr Rabbit.

"Mr Rabbit," said the little girl, "it's about my mother."

"Your mother?" said Mr Rabbit.

"It's her birthday," said the little girl.

"Happy birthday to her then," said Mr Rabbit. "What are you giving her?"

"That's just it," said the little girl. "That's why I want help. I have nothing to give her."

"Nothing to give your mother on her birthday?" said Mr Rabbit. "Little girl, you really do want help."

"I would like to give her something that she likes," said the little girl.

"Something that she likes is a good present," said Mr Rabbit.

"But what?" said the little girl.

"Yes, what?" said Mr Rabbit.

"She likes red," said the little girl.

"Red," said Mr Rabbit. "You can't give her red."

"Something red, maybe," said the little girl.

"Well," said Mr Rabbit, "there's red underwear."

"No," said the little girl, "I can't give her that."

"There are red roofs," said Mr Rabbit.

"No, we have a roof," said the little girl. "I don't want to give her that."

"There are red birds," said Mr Rabbit, "red cardinals."

"No," said the little girl, "she likes birds in trees."

"There are red fire-engines," said Mr Rabbit.

"No," said the little girl. "She doesn't like fire-engines."

"Well," said Mr Rabbit, "there are apples."

"Good," said the little girl, "that's good. She likes apples."

From *Mr Rabbit and the Lovely Present*
By CHARLOTTE ZOLOTOW

Something to think or talk about

1. Why was the little girl talking to Mr Rabbit?
2. Do you think Mr Rabbit helped?
3. Why did the little girl think an apple was a good present for her mother?
4. Why did the little girl not talk it over with her mother?
5. Look at the picture of the little girl and Mr Rabbit (page 5). How has the artist shown that one looks worried and the other doesn't?

Something to do

The rest of the story tells that the little girl wanted to give her mother more than an apple.
She talked with Mr Rabbit a little longer.
They agreed on a basket of fruit.
In the basket they put:

> something red   something yellow
> something green something blue

Think of the fruits they put in the basket.

1. Draw a picture of the little girl giving the present to her mother.

2. Draw two speech bubbles, like this:

   In one bubble write what you think the little girl said to her mother.
   In the other bubble, write what the little girl's mother said to her.

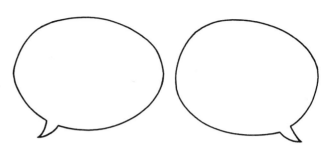

Make a birthday card.

(a) Collect all the things you will need to make a birthday card for someone in your family.
(b) Make a picture on the front, of something you think that person would like.
(c) Write a birthday message on the card.

Something to read

Look in the library for:

Title	Mr Rabbit and the Lovely Present
Author	Charlotte Zolotow
Pictures by	Maurice Sendak
Published by	Puffin

Grandma and Harry

Grandma

My grandmother's a peaceful person and she likes to sit
But there never was a grandma that was such a one to knit
     Scarves, caps, suits, socks –
     Her needles click like fifty clocks
     But not for you and not for me
     What makes her knit so busily?

                                  TED HUGHES

Is she knitting for Harry?

Harry

Harry was a white dog with black spots.
On his birthday, he got a present from Grandma.
It was a woollen sweater with roses on it.
Harry didn't like it the moment he saw it.
He didn't like the roses.
   When he tried it on, he felt cosy and snug.
But he still didn't like the roses.   He thought it was
the silliest sweater he'd ever seen.
   The next day, when Harry
went into town with the children
he wore his new sweater.
When people saw it they laughed.

When dogs saw it they barked. Harry made up his mind then and there to lose Grandma's present.

When they went into a big store to shop, the children took off his sweater and let him carry it. This was just what Harry wanted.

First he tried to lose it in the pet department, but a man found it and gave it back. Then he tried to lose it in the grocery department, but a lady found it and gave it back. Wherever Harry left it, someone found it.

In the end, Harry lost it in a very surprising way.

From *No Roses for Harry!*
By GENE ZION

Something to think or talk about

Have you ever been given something to wear that you didn't like? If so, what? Why didn't you like it?
What did you do about it?

Something to read

Title	You'll soon grow into them, Titch
Author	Pat Hutchins
Pictures by	Pat Hutchins
Published by	Picture Puffins

This is the story of a little boy whose big brother and sister gave him gifts of clothes that were too small for them.

Something to do

Draw a set of pictures of your family. Put yourself in it too.
Write the names under the pictures.
Below that, write the name of the
gift you think each person would like.
For a family of four your pictures might be set out like this:

			me
			a bicycle

Write your own ending.

How do **you** think Harry lost his sweater?

Something to read

How **did** Harry lose his sweater? Read:

Title *No Roses for Harry!*
Author *Gene Zion*
Pictures by *Margaret Bloy Graham*
Published by *Picture Puffins*

Read also the whole of the poem 'Grandma' by Ted Hughes.
You will find it in a book called *Meet My Folks*
published by Faber and Faber. It will surprise you.

Thank-you Letters

Most people like getting gifts.
Not all people like writing thank-you letters.
Do you think they should? Why?

Read these thank-you poems written by Mick Gowar.

Dear Auntie,
Oh what a nice jumper
I've always adored powder blue
and fancy you thinking of
orange and pink
for the stripes
how clever of you.

Dear Sister,
I quite understand
your concern
It's a risk sending jam
in the post
But I think I've pulled
out all the bits of
glass
So it won't taste too
sharp
spread on toast.

Dear Gran,
Many thanks for the hankies
Now I really can't wait
for the flu
and the daisies embroidered
in red round the 'M'
for Michael
how thoughtful of you.

Dear Uncle,
The soap is
terrific
so
useful
and such a kind thought
and how did you guess
that I'd just used the
last of
the soap that last
Christmas brought?

Dear Cousin,
What socks!
and the same sort you wear
so they must be
the last word in style
and I'm certain you're right
that the luminous green
will make me stand out
a mile.

Dear Grandad,
Don't fret
I'm delighted
so don't think your gift
will offend
I'm not at all hurt
that you gave up this year
and just sent me
a fiver
to spend.

Something to think or talk about

Have you learned anything about Mick from reading his letters? If so, what?

Which do you like best:

      (a) getting a wrapped gift,

or   (b) getting money to buy a gift for yourself? (Give reasons.)

Something to do

1. Ask ten friends whether they like
   (a) or (b) better.
   Put their answers in a chart like this:

name of friend	getting a wrapped gift	getting money
1 Sheila	✓	
2 Keith		✓
3		
4		
5		
6		
7		
8		
9		
10		

Compare your chart with other charts from your group.

2. Make a coloured picture of each of the gifts Mick got.

3. Write a thank-you letter to someone who has given you a gift at some time.

Gift Lists

Some people make gift lists. Here is one.

My Christmas List

A police car
A helicopter
A gun that goes pop
A Frisbee
A ball
An Action Man that won't stop
A torch
A guitar
A printing set with ink
A bouncer
A new bear
A submarine that won't sink
A sword
A typewriter
A stove so I can cook
A radio
A Wendy house
Another dinosaur book –
Of course, Father Christmas, it's clearly understood
That I'll only get all of this if I'm specially good.

Gyles Brandreth

Something to think or talk about

1. What is the title of the poem?

2. Who is the author?

3. Do you think gift lists are a good idea? (Give reasons.)

4. What other gift lists might people make?

Something to do

The poem lists eighteen things.
Write a list of eighteen things **you** would like.
Now try to write **your** list as a poem.

Look at 'My Christmas List'.
There are four pairs of rhyming words. What are they?
The first one – **pop** – is at the end of line 3.
At the end of which lines do the other rhyming words come?
You may have to change the order of the words in your list
to get rhymes that will fit.

Use the last two lines of Gyles Brandreth's poem
to finish your own.

A Gift for a Friend

You could use junk to make a gift for a friend.
Here are two ideas.

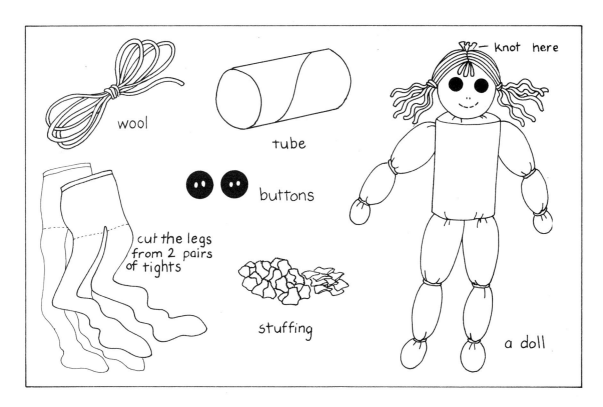

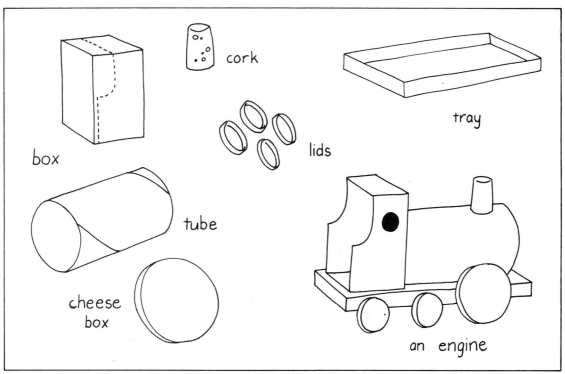

Make your own Wrapping Paper

You will need
newsprint or other thin paper
a small potato
a knife
a plate and a piece of foam sponge
some soft paint
a pad of newspaper

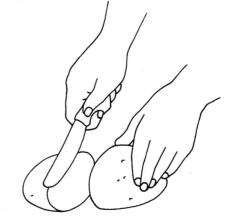

What to do

1. Cut your potato in half.

2. Put the sponge on the plate.

3. Squeeze some soft paint over your sponge.

4. Lay your sheet of newsprint flat on top of your pad of newspaper.

5. Press the half-potato on the sponge.

6. Print the shape on the newsprint, like this.

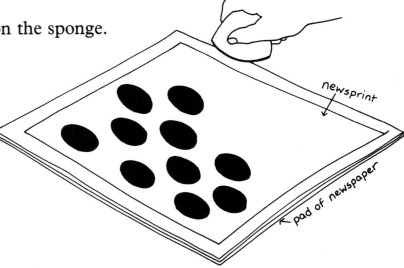

More wrapping paper

You might now like to try two shapes and two colours.

What to do

Cut your other half potato into the shape of a triangle.

Using two colours, print like this   or   like this

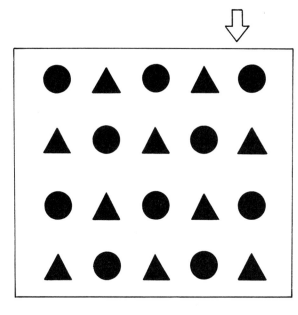 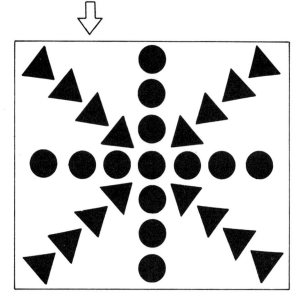

Make a bow for your parcel.

You will need: 4 strips of paper, the length
                    of a page of this book and 1cm wide
              scissors
              glue or stapler

What to do   1. Fix each strip like this.      (glue or staple)

2. Use strips 1 and 2 to make a cross.    3. Add strips 3 and 4.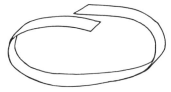

4. Wrap your parcel.   Fix the bow on top.

Gifts of a Different Kind

Would you think it strange to give a gift to
someone you don't know?
Many people give in this way.
They are saddened by something they have
read in a newspaper or heard on radio or television.
They wish to help.

Read this poem about children who lived
more than a hundred years ago.

Street Children

Street children –
Hungry, tired,
Piteous children –
Looking for a place to sleep –
Street children.

Roaming the streets at night,
Sleeping in barrows and bins,
Longing for a home and a bed –
Street children.

Children living in poverty,
Eating any scraps,
No one picks and chooses –
Street children.

AMANDA THOMSON

Something to think about

How did you feel when you read the poem?

A young man was so upset when he heard about street children that he made up his mind to do something to help them.

His name was Tom Barnardo, a name that is known to many people today.

Have you heard of him?
Have you seen the name *Barnardo* anywhere?

Read his story on page 20.

This old photograph shows some of Tom Barnardo's boys learning to be carpenters.

Tom Barnardo

Dr Barnardo

In the year 1866 a young man, Tom Barnardo, started a school for poor boys in London. The school was an old donkey shed and soon it was crowded with boys who wanted to learn to read.

One night a new pupil, Jim Jarvis, stayed behind. He was one of the street children. He asked if he could stay the night at the school.

"You can't do that," said Tom. "Where do you usually sleep?"

"Come and I'll show you," said Jim.

It was midnight when he led Tom to the Rag Market. Jim and Tom scrambled up the wall of an old building. At the top, under the roof, were lots of homeless boys. It was a sight Tom never forgot.

Tom became a doctor. He made up his mind that no child should ever be homeless.

Friends gave him gifts of money and helped him to set up Dr Barnardo's Homes. Although there are no street children today, there are still many children who need to be cared for in special homes.

Some of the homeless boys helped by Tom Barnardo.

Without gifts of money these homes would have to close. Perhaps you have seen a Dr Barnardo's shop. It sells second-hand things gifted by people who no longer use them. Perhaps you have heard an appeal on television for gifts of money.

Perhaps *you* can help.

Something to think and talk about

Here are some groups who help other people. They need gifts of money to help with the work they are doing.

Now read page 22 to find out more.

How can we help?

Something to do along with your group

Below are addresses of eight groups who help others.
Choose one or two you would like to find out about.
Write to them.   You will get replies.
They will tell you about the work
the groups do.   They will also tell you how
you can help.

Royal Society for the Protection of Birds
Dept. LBS2
The Lodge
Sandy
Bedfordshire

National Children's Home
85 Highbury Park
London N5 1UD

Royal National Institute for the Blind
224 Great Portland Street
London W1N 6AA

Royal Society for the Prevention of Cruelty to Animals
Headquarters
Causeway
Horsham
Sussex RH12 1HG

Royal National Institute for the Deaf
Room DB
105 Gower Street
London WC1E 6AH

Oxfam
Room WC01
Freepost
Oxford OX2 7BR

Save the Children
17 Grove Lane
London SE5 8RD

Dr Barnardo's
Tanners Lane
Barkingside
Ilford
Essex 1G6 1 QG

Something to think about, talk about and do

When replies arrive, look through them quickly.
Read headings.   Study pictures.   Read bits that
interest you.

Perhaps you can think of a way to
help one of the groups.

Here are some ideas to discuss with
your teacher.

Glossary

adored	liked very much
appeal	request for help
author	someone who writes books, plays, poems
cardinal	bird (19 cm long) found in North America
concern	worry
department	part of a shop
embroidered	decorated by needle and thread
fret	be unhappy
grocery	food
junk	things no longer needed
luminous	glowing in the dark
offend	hurt someone's feelings
piteous	that you feel sorry for
public	people
publishers	producers of books, newspapers, magazines
refused	would not do it
replies	answers
rhymes	words with the same sound
second-hand	already used by someone
style	fashion
sweater	pullover

Make your own glossary from the story below.

It's Christmas Eve. The tree in the corner of the room shimmers as a rush of air catches the tinsel draped around it.

Mysterious parcels lie at the base of the tree. They have been turned over, shaken, prodded and even smelt in a vain attempt to discover the contents.

Tomorrow all will be revealed. The once tidy room will be littered with Christmas wrapping paper, ribbons, cards, games, toys and sweets. But who cares?

Happy Christmas!

REVIEW

Did you enjoy this book?
If you did, which parts did you like best?
Were there any parts you didn't enjoy?
If so, which, and why?

Can you remember your answer to the question 'What is a gift?' (page 3)
Would you still give the same answer?
If not, what would you say now?

Quiz

Without looking back, try to answer these questions.

1. What would you find on the title page of a book?
2. What would you find in the contents list?
3. What is a glossary?
4. When you were asked to find a book to read (pages 7 and 9), what were you told about it?
5. Did you read any of the books you were asked to find?
    If you did, what would you tell your friends about them?

Glossary

How many words did you put in your glossary?
Check with friends.   Did they have more or fewer?

Did they choose the same words?

Did you remember to put the words in the order
of the alphabet?